OPTICAL ILLUSIONS
ACTIVITY BOOK

ARCTURUS

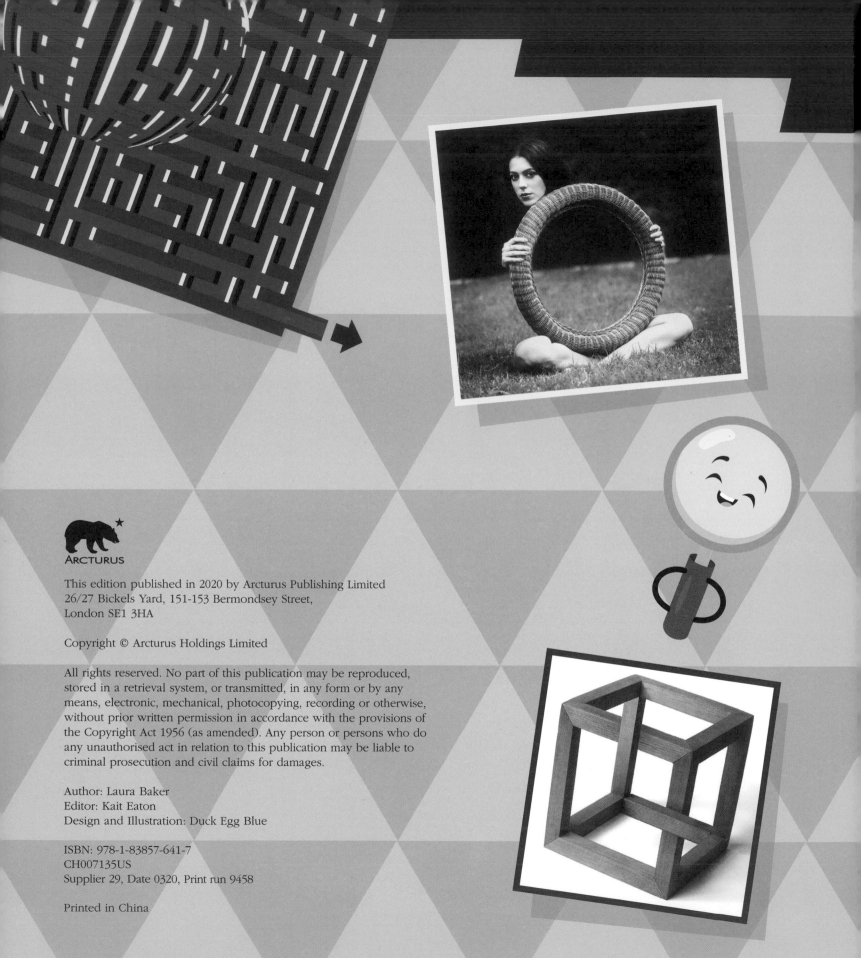

ARCTURUS

This edition published in 2020 by Arcturus Publishing Limited
26/27 Bickels Yard, 151-153 Bermondsey Street,
London SE1 3HA

Author: Laura Baker
Editor: Kait Eaton
Design and Illustration: Duck Egg Blue

ISBN: 978-1-83857-641-7
CH007135US
Supplier 29, Date 0320, Print run 9458

Printed in China

CONTENTS

INTRODUCTION

You can always trust your eyes and what they show you, right? Wrong! Your peepers work very hard to see the world around you, but sometimes they can be tricked into seeing things that aren't there.

Optical illusions do just this. They are pictures designed to fool you. Sometimes they work by playing with your brain's interpretation of the image. And sometimes they confuse your eyes as they jump around to make sense of a picture.

Learn all about different types of optical illusions in this book, and then get involved in the brain-boggling! Pick up your pens and follow the instructions to make your own illusions to fool your friends.

UNBELIEVABLE EFFECTS!

The bamboozling begins now ...

CHAPTER 1
MOVING PICTURES

The optical illusions in this section might make you dizzy! Even though you know it's impossible that they can be moving on the page, you see otherwise, and the pictures shift before your very eyes. Have a look and see for yourself—but take a break if you start to feel seasick!

PULSING PATTERNS

Look into the **center** of these pictures.
Do you see them **pulsating** and **moving outward**?

WOW! WHAT'S HAPPENING?

Your eyes make tiny, fast, jerky movements to try and make sense of this image. Your brain takes in so much information as your eyes dart around that it gets confused and thinks the picture is moving instead of your eyes!

Carefully color in the blank squares in the white pattern above. Can you see it start to move, too?

SPINNING SHAPES

How can ink on a page seem to travel around and around?
These illusions will really get you **in a spin!**

Can you focus on the moving pictures long enough to spot seven differences?

WOW! WHAT'S HAPPENING?

Scientists think that the contrast between dark and light colors next to each other makes these images look like they're spinning. Do you see the inner circle spinning counterclockwise and the middle circle spinning clockwise? Look closely at where the black line is on each zigzag. This affects the direction you perceive.

Cover half of the image with your hand and see the **spinning slow down** or **even stop!**

WOW! WHAT'S HAPPENING?

Covering part of the picture takes away the overload of information sent to your brain and helps you focus on one section.

WACKY WHEELS

This one is wheel-y **mind-bending**! Watch the Ferris wheel **spin around** as if it were real. But how?

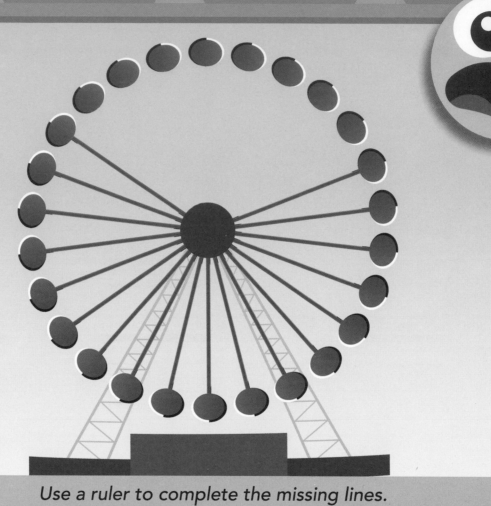

Use a ruler to complete the missing lines. Do you see the whole wheel spinning?

WOW! WHAT'S HAPPENING?

Once again, the contrast between colors on this picture tricks your brain into thinking the wheel is moving. The black lines on one edge of each car make the picture seem to spin clockwise.

Color your own **moving wheels**! Can you make these gears spin?
Follow the number key below.

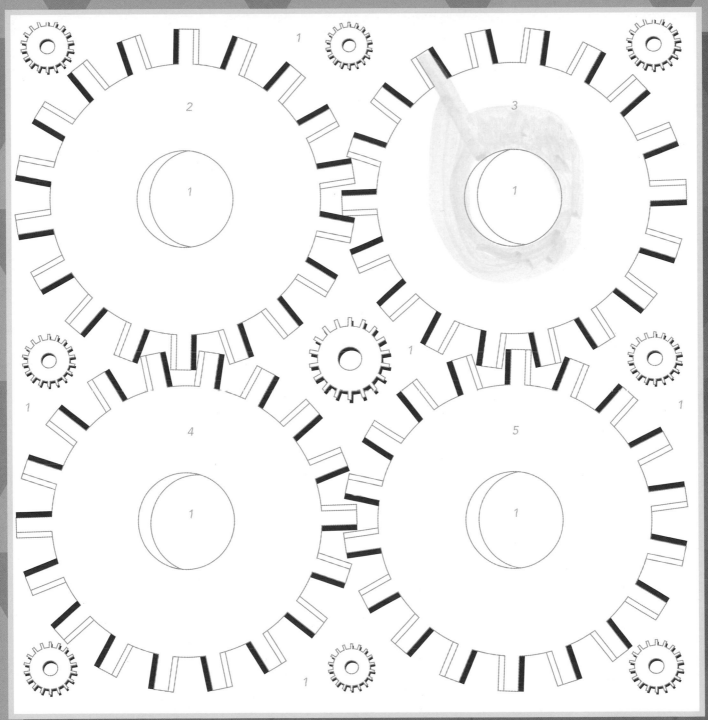

1 = Yellow   2 = Blue   3 = Pink   4 = Purple   5 = Green

SHOCKING SPIRALS

Spiral illusions can really shock you. Some are **real spirals**, and some only give that **illusion**! See if you can figure out if these pictures are **spirals** or a series of **concentric circles**.

Follow the black line with your finger. Is it a real spiral?

Use a black pen to fill in the gray lines to complete this picture. Can you see the spiral illusion?

The black bars are arranged in concentric circles.

WOW! WHAT'S HAPPENING?

In the first picture, the contrast and closeness of the circles make it really hard for your eyes and brain to follow the lines. In the second picture, the angle of each line leads your eyes inward. But actually, there is no spiral there! The black lines are arranged in concentric circles.

WOBBLING WAVES

This one might actually make you **feel seasick**! Can you see the wavy lines **rippling** like waves on the sea?

WOW! WHAT'S HAPPENING?

The waves in this picture seem to ripple as your eyes pass over them. The tiny movements your eyes make as they process the contrasting black and white stripes give this illusion of movement.

Draw your own moving waves! You can create variations on this illusion with a simple homemade template. You'll need a piece of cardstock, a piece of paper, a pencil, and a black pen.

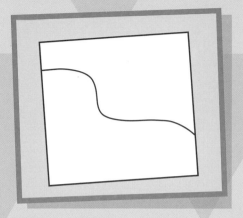

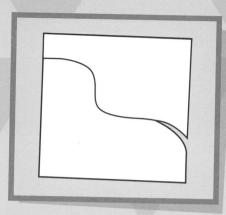

❶ Draw a long wavy line on a piece of card.

❷ Ask an adult to help you carefully cut along this line. The cut cardstock is now your template.

❸ Place your template near the bottom of a piece of paper. Trace the wavy line on to the paper with pencil.

❹ Move the template up about 1/8 inch. Trace the line again. Repeat until you have covered the page with a pattern of wavy lines.

❺ Color every other stripe in black or a dark color. Erase any pencil marks you can see. Are your waves rippling now?

Cool wave effect!

Try moving your template up at an angle, so the stripes get wider on one side as you go. This gives an even greater illusion of depth!

EERIE EYES

Do you ever feel like you're being watched? You will with these eerie illusions! As you cast your eyes over them, you should feel the eyes on the page **shifting back and forth**.

Eye, eye. What's this?

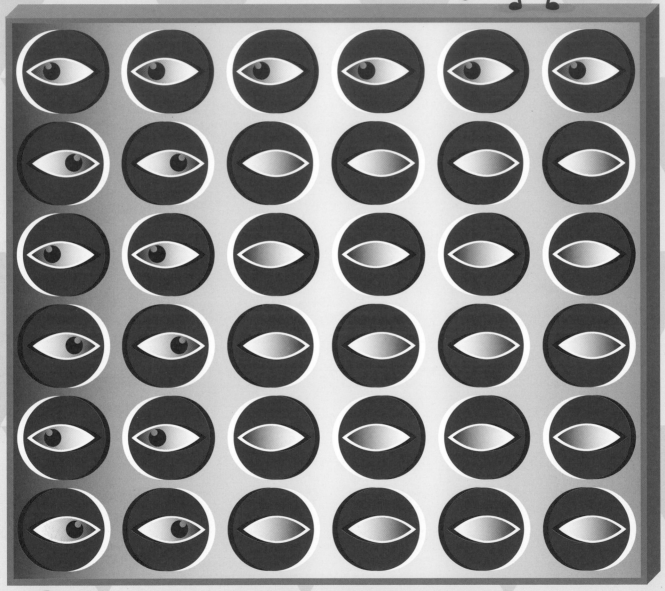

Draw in the missing pupils, making sure to follow the pattern. Can you feel the eyes on the page watching you?

Color this pattern to complete the mesmerizing effect. Now look at the image and see how the pattern draws you in toward the eye, then back to the pattern, then in toward the eye again!

WOW! WHAT'S HAPPENING?

The repeated and contrasting patterns fool your brain into thinking something is moving as your eyes take in the pictures. On top of that, humans are drawn to eyes, so these illusions really pull us in.

FLOATING FUN

This book is made of single sheets of paper, each one layer only. So how can it look like this image has something floating on top of it?

Find your way from the top to the bottom of this maze. Can you make it through the floating ball in the middle?

WOW! WHAT'S HAPPENING?

The change in pattern between the background and the ball makes the ball look like it's on a different level to the background behind. Watch the ball while moving your head from side to side. Do you see it seem to float even farther over the background?

MAKE A FLOATING FINGER!

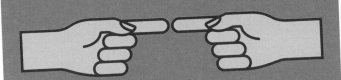

1 Place the tips of your index fingers together horizontally. Hold them about 6in in front of your face, at eye level.

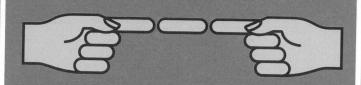

2 Focus on your fingers. Then, move your eyes to look at something past your fingers, about a yard or two away. A floating finger should appear!

3 Try moving your fingers closer and farther apart to change the size of the floating finger.

WOW! WHAT'S HAPPENING?

Focus on an object, then cover your eyes one at a time. Do you see the image in front of you move from side to side? Each eye sees slightly differently. When you focus on something in the distance, your brain overlaps the eyes' two images in the foreground. In this case, that creates a floating finger!

GROWING

How can a picture on a page seem to **grow without stopping**?
Take a look at these pictures to find out ... Go on, grow for it!

WOW! WHAT'S HAPPENING?

This pattern works hard to confuse you. First, the contrasting colors baffle your brain. Then, the pointed lines and shading in the center section lead your eyes outward. Your brain is already so confused that it believes the whole picture is moving!

Color the heart in the middle of these lines black, as dark as you can. Does it seem to grow when you stare at it now?

WOW! WHAT'S HAPPENING?

Do you see how the black lines closest to the heart are wider than the lines farther out? They create narrow white gaps that your brain tries to fill in. To do this, it uses the black of the shape in the center, making the heart look like it's expanding.

SHRINKING

The longer you stare at them, the more shrinking illusions seem to **shrink away from you**. Can you make people shrink, too?

Find a path through this shrinking pattern, from the outside to the inside.

WOW! WHAT'S HAPPENING?

Just like the growing illusions, the contrasting colors and sharp points confuse your brain and lead your eyes. In this case, the black shading on the outside of the blue stripes gives a shrinking effect.

Make a shrinking machine! Follow the steps to make a spinner that gives the illusion of your friends shrinking away from you. You will need a piece of cardstock, a black pen, and a sharp pencil.

1 Draw a large circle onto a piece of cardstock and carefully cut it out.

2 Draw a spiral pattern on to your circle, as shown. Color it in with a black pen, then ask an adult to help you push a sharp pencil through the middle of the card, tip down.

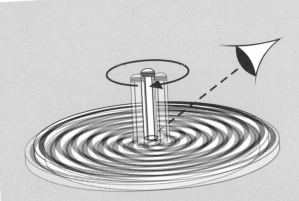

3 Using the pencil, spin your top clockwise. Stare at the center of the spiral and count to 30.

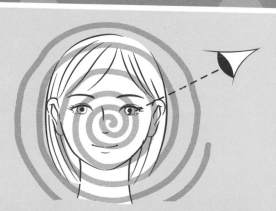

4 Quickly look at your friend. They should appear to be shrinking away from you!

Try spinning the top counterclockwise and follow step 4 again. Does your friend seem to be growing now?

OP ART

Optical art—or op art, for short—is art that uses strongly **contrasting lines and shapes** that can create optical illusions. It was so popular at one time that even famous artists got involved!

Color each band marked with a dot using a black pen. Can you see the image coming out of the page now?

WOW! WHAT'S HAPPENING?

This fence, inspired by op artist Victor Vasarely, uses the contrast of the metal against the background to play with your eyes. The clever shaping of the bars gives the illusion that shapes are coming out toward you—when in fact, they're flat!

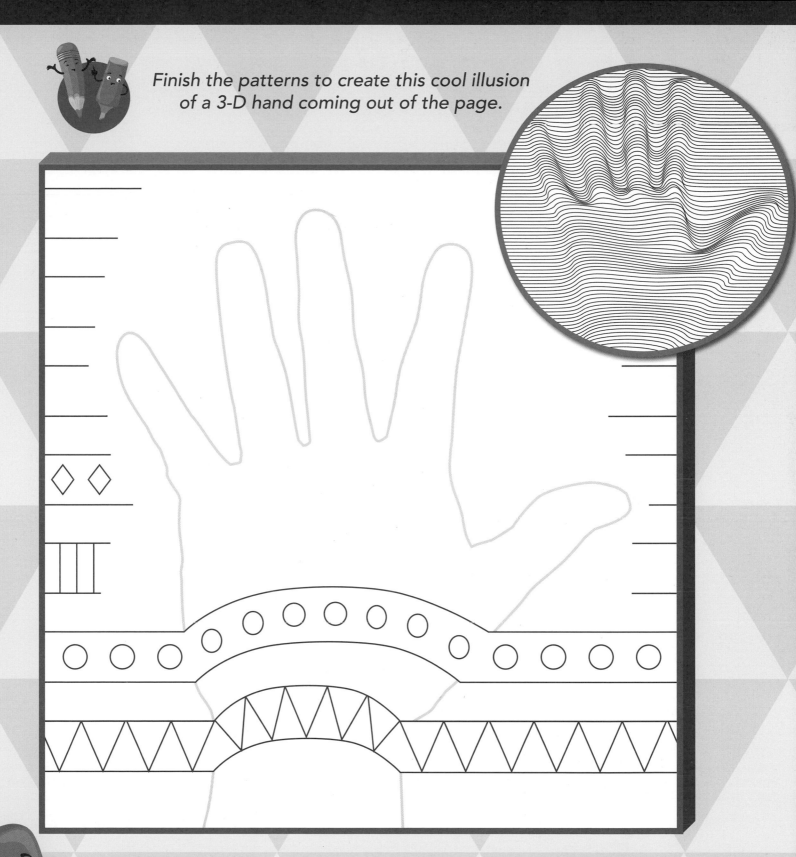

Finish the patterns to create this cool illusion of a 3-D hand coming out of the page.

Keep your patterns straight on the horizontal lines that meet up with the hand. But on the hand itself, make sure your patterns curve up around the hand shape to build the 3-D illusion.

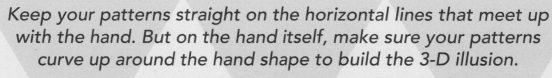

ROLLING AWAY

Be careful or this ball might **roll away** from you!
Or will it? Maybe it's all a floating, moving illusion ...

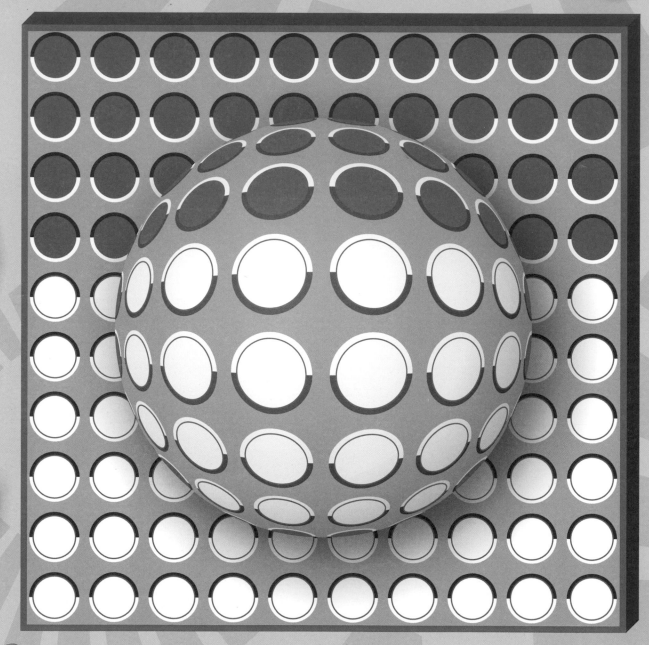

*Color in the white dots to finish the picture. Can you see the
ball rolling up the page and the background sliding down?*

CHAPTER 2
TRICKED YOU!

All optical illusions are designed to trick your eyes and brain. But the illusions in this section go a step further. They give you more than meets the eye ... Look closely to see if you can figure them out. Then, try to trick your friends!

SNEAKY SHAPES

What do you see when you look at this image? Is it a pattern of **circles**, **triangles,** or **curved, six-pointed stars**? Keep looking and you will probably change your mind!

Look carefully at the pattern again. Can you find a hidden pathway from the top to the bottom? It's tricky to see, but it is definitely there!

Do you see stacks of cubes or a pattern of six-pointed stars in the image below?

 Use your pens and pencils to make each cube a different color. Do you still see the stars?

WOW! WHAT'S HAPPENING?

These illusions show how flexible our brains can be. We can view these images in several different ways, so our brain flips between them as it tries to understand exactly what we see. Adding color to the picture helps your brain see the cubes much more clearly than the stars. In fact, it's quite difficult to see the stars at all once the cubes are colored!

CIRCLE CONFUSION

You know what a perfect circle looks like, right? But how can you be sure when a **perplexing pattern** gets in the way?

WOW! WHAT'S HAPPENING?

These may not look like circles, but they are, in fact, perfectly round! The patterns in the background and on the circles themselves confuse your brain into thinking the rings are wobbly.

Create your own confusing curves! Use a compass, a protractor, a ruler, and a pen to draw a circle out of straight lines.

❶ Use a compass to draw a perfect circle on a piece of paper. If you don't have a compass, trace a large mug or glass instead.

❷ Use a protractor to measure and mark every 10° on your circle, as shown. If you don't have a protractor, use a ruler to measure equal distances all around the circle.

❸ Start at the mark bottom center. Count nine marks to the right. Connect these two marks with a straight line.

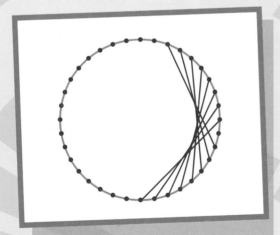

❹ Move to the mark to the right of the one where you started. Connect it with the one just past the mark where you finished in step 3. Continue drawing lines like this all around the circle, as shown.

Now that your lines are part of a bigger circle, do they still look straight? Do you see how you've created a second perfect circle on the inside ring?

DOT DECEPTION

These illusions are **masters of deception**! You will see dots that aren't there, colors that aren't right ... Are you going dotty yet?

Move your eyes around this picture. How many dots can you count?

WOW! WHAT'S HAPPENING?

There are actually no dots at all in this image, but as you move your eyes around the picture, dots seem to appear and disappear at the corners between squares. Your eyes are tricked by the contrast between the red squares and white lines, and they see spots that aren't there!

WOW! WHAT'S HAPPENING?

Would you believe that the dots below are gray? The longer you look, the more they seem green! The purple and red design takes over and gives the dots a wash of red light. In that red tinge, your brain sees them as green.

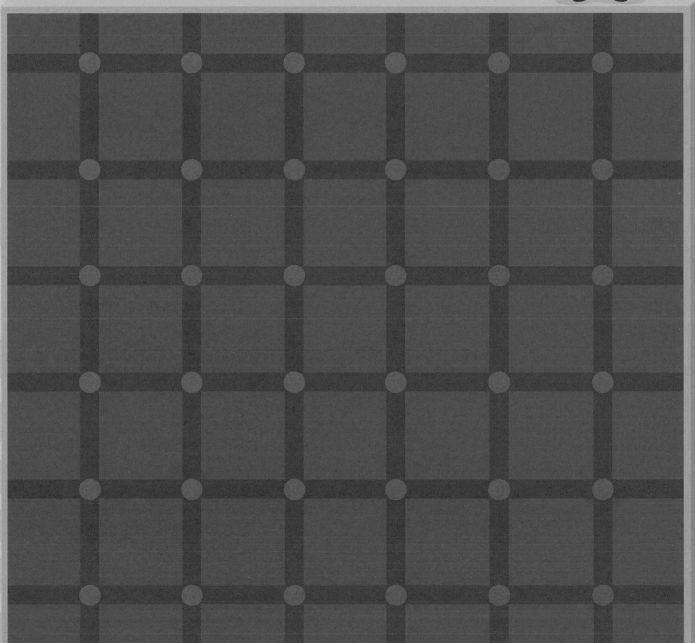

SIZE DISGUISE

Try these illusions on for size! The **context** of the objects in these pictures plays tricks on your brain. Size them up and see for yourself!

1 Blue dot

A ☐

B ☐

In each pair of pictures, which do you think is bigger: A or B?

2 Blue ring

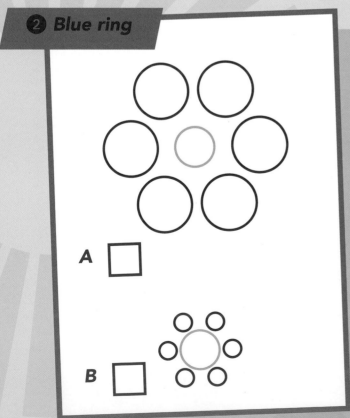

A ☐

B ☐

3 Blue lines

A ☐

B ☐

④ Arches

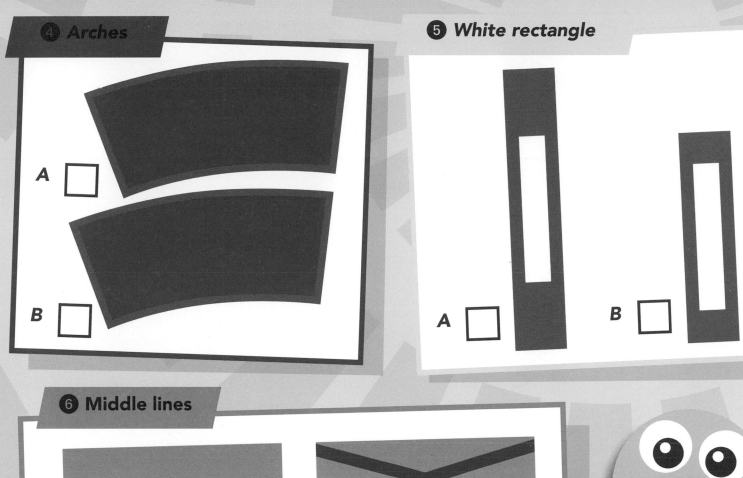

A ☐

B ☐

⑤ White rectangle

A ☐　　　B ☐

⑥ Middle lines

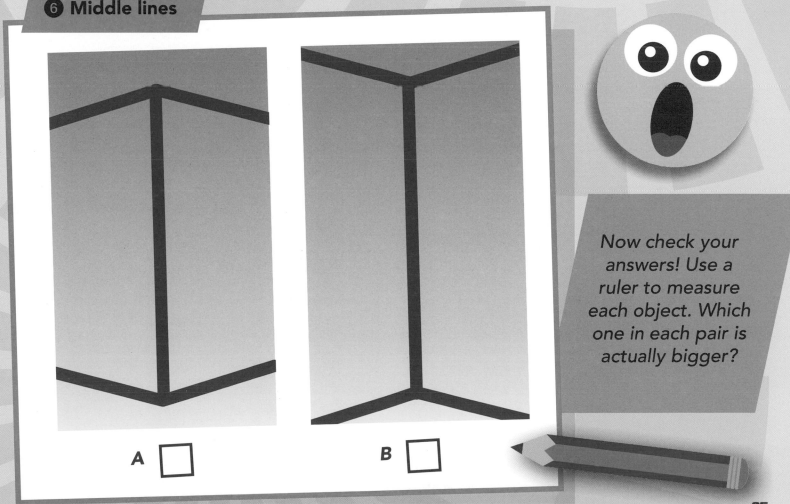

A ☐　　　B ☐

Now check your answers! Use a ruler to measure each object. Which one in each pair is actually bigger?

TILTING LINES

Do these lines look lined up to you? Are they straight or wonky? It's hard to tell with other lines confusing your eyes and brain.

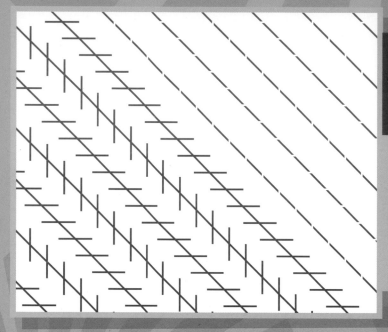

WOW! WHAT'S HAPPENING?

The long lines are parallel to each other, but once you add the short marks, the lines don't look parallel anymore! The different angles of these shorter lines make the longer ones look like they're tilting.

Finish the pattern of short lines. What happens to the long lines?

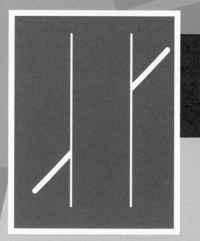

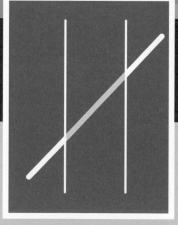

WOW! WHAT'S HAPPENING?

This illusion confuses even scientists! They think that the angle of the diagonal line against the vertical tricks your brain into believing that the line on the other side should be lower than it really is.

Do the diagonal lines in the first picture look lined up? Use a ruler to find out.

Use a black felt-tip pen to carefully color in each shape marked with a dot. Do the horizontal lines still look level?

WOW! WHAT'S HAPPENING?

You saw that the lines were perfectly parallel, but then why do they look wonky now that the rectangles are colored in? The zigzag pattern of rectangles makes the lines seem unbalanced, and your brain sees this as the lines leaning in toward each other.

PERSPECTIVE POWER

Can you sort out the sizes of these silhouettes? Do those photos look right to you? It's all a **matter of perspective** ...

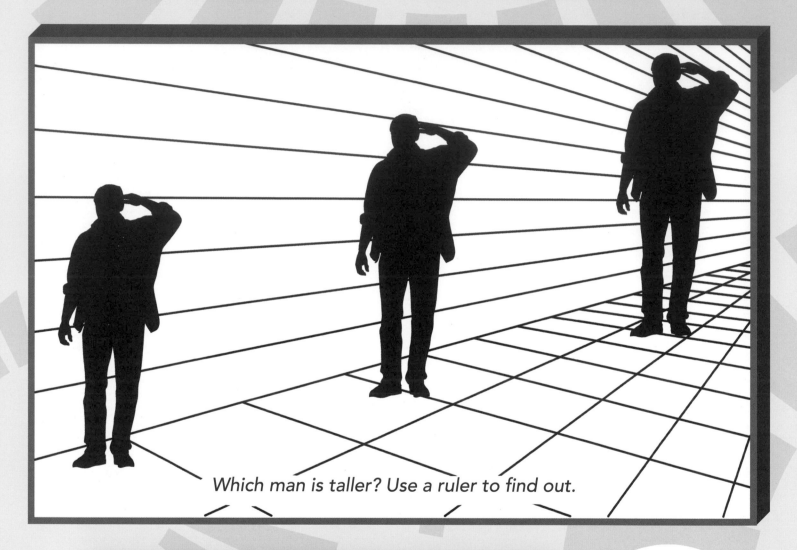

Which man is taller? Use a ruler to find out.

WOW! WHAT'S HAPPENING?

Did you discover that all three men are exactly the same height? The perspective lines in the background suggest distance, fooling your brain into thinking that the man on the right is farther away and therefore taller in relation to the man on the left.

Play with perspective to create a trick photo!

In the pictures below, the people are positioned just right to make it look like the flower is huge and the woman is holding up a small Leaning Tower of Pisa.

WOW! WHAT'S HAPPENING?

Perspective is the way 3-D objects are shown on a flat surface, often using lines and depth to convey relative size. If we play with those lines and depth, our brains get very confused!

Follow these steps to make your own trick photo!

1 Start with a person or object close to the camera.

2 Then, position another person or object in the distance behind. Move the camera until these line up exactly.

3 Then capture that perfect shot. Click!

COLOR QUIZ

Color yourself clever! Can you name the colors below quicker than a friend? Don't be fooled by the **conflicting** words and pictures ...

RED	GREEN	ORANGE	BLACK	PINK	BLUE	GREEN
BLUE	YELLOW	GREEN	YELLOW	WHITE	PURPLE	BLACK
WHITE	GREEN	PINK	BLUE	ORANGE	BLUE	PINK
RED	YELLOW	ORANGE	BLACK	WHITE	ORANGE	PURPLE
PINK	GREEN	BLUE	PURPLE	PINK	YELLOW	BLUE

Time how long it takes you to say all the colors of these squares correctly—
NOT the words written inside them.

WOW! WHAT'S HAPPENING?

Your brain can't help reading the words as it goes along. But then it's processing two things at once: the color it sees and the word it reads. That's too much information! Your brain gets confused and needs extra time to think about what is really there.

YELLOW	PINK	ORANGE	PURPLE	BLACK	GREEN	PINK
RED	GREEN	YELLOW	BLACK	ORANGE	BLUE	RED
BLACK	BLUE	WHITE	GREEN	BLACK	YELLOW	BLUE
YELLOW	PINK	ORANGE	PURPLE	WHITE	RED	PINK
GREEN	ORANGE	BLUE	RED	BLACK	BLUE	YELLOW

Now time a friend. Who is the fastest at getting through them correctly?

INVISIBLE SHAPES

These illusions are cleverly designed to make you see things that aren't there. The **invisible** is shaping up to be visible after all!

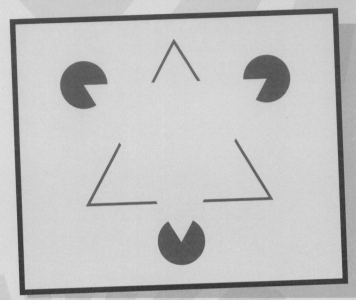

Draw in all the missing shapes.

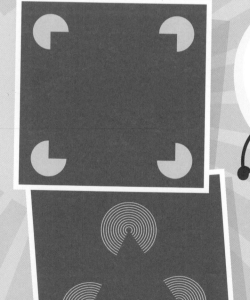

WOW! WHAT'S HAPPENING?

Your brain fills in the missing shapes quite easily. It takes clues from the images that it can see and fills in the gaps using previous knowledge of shapes. For example, in the top image, it connects the three points cut out of each wedge into a triangle shape.

Draw your own invisible shapes!

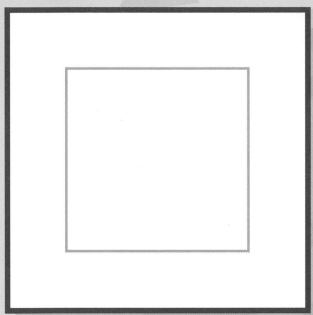

1 Start by drawing a square shape lightly in pencil. From now on, avoid drawing anything inside this shape.

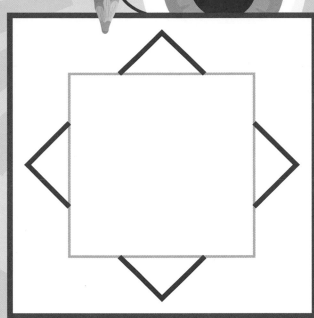

2 Then draw another square at 45° in felt-tip pen over the top, avoiding the pencil square area.

3 Draw solid shapes or patterns around the corners of the original square in felt-tip pen.

4 Remove the pencil marks of the original square. Now see if a friend can see the invisible shape you had in mind!

PHONY FACES

These faces are just upside down ... or are they? Look closer to see if your brain has been fooled by **phony photos**.

Turn the page upside down. What do you notice?

WOW! WHAT'S HAPPENING?

When a face is the right way up, your brain takes it in all at once. When it's upside down, your brain looks at each part individually. If the eyes, the mouth, and the nose all look fine on their own, your brain adds this up to a normal face. But turn the page upside down and you'll see that it's not normal at all! Some of the features have, in fact, been flipped in these mind-bending illusions.

Spot five differences between these tricky, topsy-turvy pictures.

CAN IT BE 3-D?

On a flat page, you can't really see something in 3-D, unless it's a pop-up piece or virtual reality. But these illusions trick you into thinking something might be **coming out of the page**. Can it be?

WOW! WHAT'S HAPPENING?

This picture is made to look as if the elephant is walking right out of the frame. Clever use of perspective and the realism of the elephant fool your brain into seeing the 3-D effect. The elephant is interacting with the frame itself, too—its back feet are on the inside and its front feet have come all the way out!

Can you draw the frame this man is holding onto as he steps out of the picture? What do you think he might be escaping from? Draw the scene he is fleeing inside the frame.

47

TRICK YOUR SENSES

Your sight isn't the only sense that can be fooled. Find a friend and try tricking your sense of touch with this simple test.

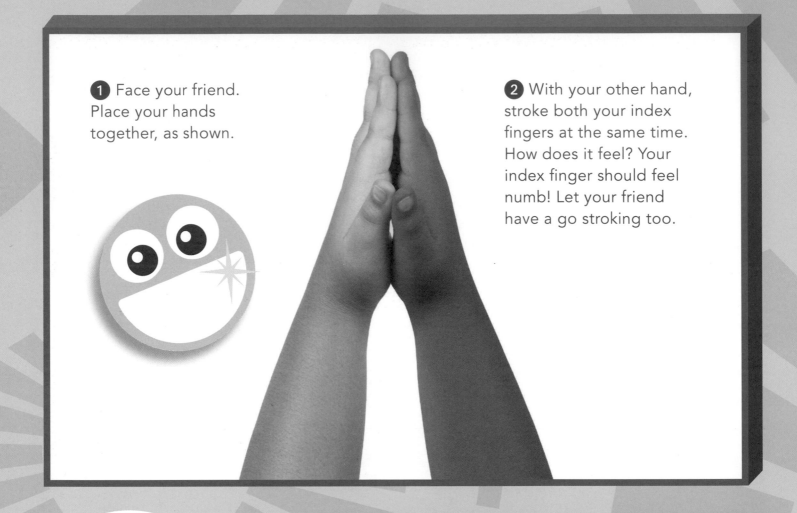

1 Face your friend. Place your hands together, as shown.

2 With your other hand, stroke both your index fingers at the same time. How does it feel? Your index finger should feel numb! Let your friend have a go stroking too.

WOW! WHAT'S HAPPENING?

Because you can't feel the stroking sensation on your friend's index finger, your brain doesn't expect you to feel the sensation on the other finger in the pair either. You end up with a strange, numb sensation—even though you know you can feel touch just fine!

CHAPTER 3
THAT'S IMPOSSIBLE!

The illusions you've seen so far are mind-bending, but once you look at them closely, you can usually make sense of them. Not so in this chapter! The more you look at the illusions here, the more you'll realize they can't actually exist at all. Prepare for your brain to be boggled!

TRICKY TRIANGLE

One of the best-known impossible shapes, the **Penrose triangle**, will drive you around the bend as you try to figure it out. Can you create one to confuse a friend?

Trace these triangles with your finger. Do they work? Try building one with blocks or dice. Can you do it?

WOW! WHAT'S HAPPENING?

This shape looks like a 3-D triangle, but as you follow it around, you notice that at each corner, one side disappears behind the next. The angles just don't work! As a 3-D object, this triangle could not exist.

Draw your own tricky triangle to fool your friends, using lines, circles, and sneaky shading.

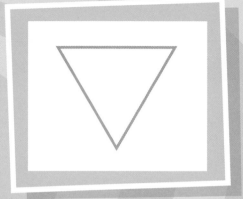

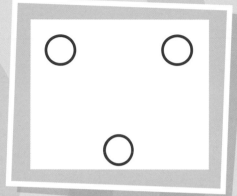

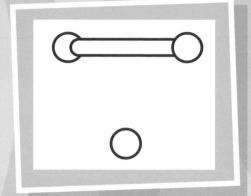

1 With your pencil, lightly draw a triangle with three equal sides as a guide. Position the triangle with the flat edge at the top.

2 Draw a circle in each corner. These will become spheres. Erase your triangle guide.

3 Draw a tube from the top left circle to the top right circle. This tube should leave from the center of the left circle and end at the edge of the right circle, as shown. Round the end of the tube on the first circle for a 3-D effect.

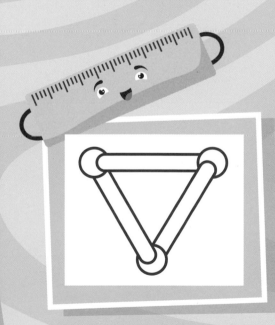

4 Repeat step 3, drawing a tube down from the top right circle to the bottom circle. Repeat again from the bottom to the top left.

5 Color in each tube with a felt-tip pen, making sure to color over the circle line that the tube overlaps.

6 Add shading to the same side of each sphere and tube to finish the 3-D effect.

IMPOSSIBLE SHAPES

Working in the same way as the tricky triangle, all kinds of impossible shapes can be created. The **impossibilities are endless!**

WOW! WHAT'S HAPPENING?

Like the Penrose triangle, these shapes can't exist in 3-D. They look like they should work—the shapes themselves are normal enough—but corners and lines are in the wrong positions.

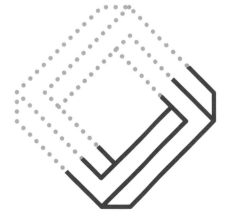

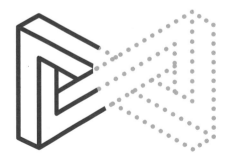

Trace the dotted lines to reveal each impossible figure.

MODEL MAGIC

Look closely at these pictures. Could they exist in real life as 3-D models? No—they're a **model of impossibility**!

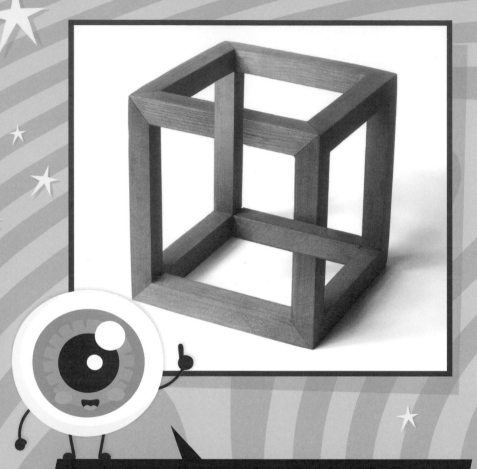

Draw a normal cube like this one with a pencil.

WOW! WHAT'S HAPPENING?

These pictures play tricks with perspective, shading, and your brain's expectations of how objects should work. This cube, for example, has bars that pass behind others where they shouldn't. In a real-life model, the bars would have to bend to go around the others, but the picture shows them as straight. Your brain wants to believe the cube is real so it gets very confused trying to figure it out!

Now erase the top front bars, as shown, and redraw them so they appear to go behind the rear bars. You've made the cube impossible!

Color the blank squares red to see this impossible model.

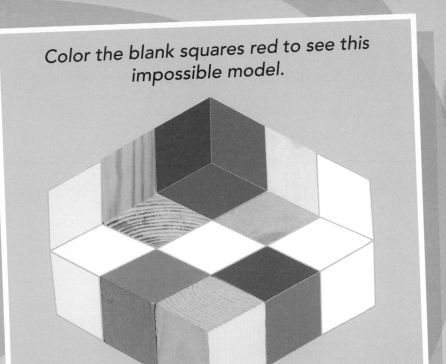

Does the structure below make sense?

Follow the trail with your finger: Start at the top of the ladder. Move left to the tree. Turn down to the bottom of the ladder. Are you still on the same level? Then how is the man climbing up? It's impossible!

STAIRS TO NOWHERE

Do you ever feel like you're going around in circles and getting nowhere? You will with these **impossible stairs**!

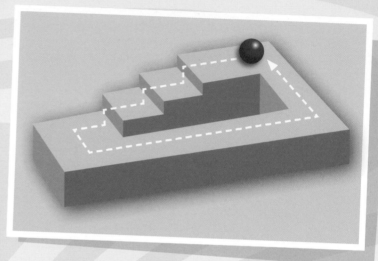

Trace the paths down these stairs. Do they make sense?

WOW! WHAT'S HAPPENING?

Have you figured out that these stairs are in an endless loop? You'd be traveling downstairs forever if you tried to walk on them! Clever perspective and shadowing on the images make all the staircases seem to travel downward when you follow them around, but you know that's not possible. They need a beginning and end!

WOW! WHAT'S HAPPENING?

Artist István Orosz combined different perspectives to make this impossible picture. Do you see how the people standing on the back wall make that wall look flat like the ground? Do you notice how people seem to go both up and down the large front staircase? It all works together to make it impossible to figure out where the stairs go!

UNREAL PERSPECTIVE

Put it into perspective ... except that you can't with these tricky pics!
See what happens when you **mix perspectives**. It's unreal!

Color in the two shadows in this picture. Is the gray strip a road or a wall?

WOW! WHAT'S HAPPENING?

The shadow of the man on the left appears to bend
upward, making the gray strip look like a wall. But
the shadow of the man on the right implies that he is
walking across a road. This mix of perspectives in the
same space makes an impossible picture!

This photo uses two different perspectives to raise questions. Where is the ground? Could this be a room in real life? What do you think?

Create your own perplexing perspective illusion!

❶ Find a shoebox and glue items to the bottom, such as dollhouse furniture or chairs made of cardboard. Leave to dry.

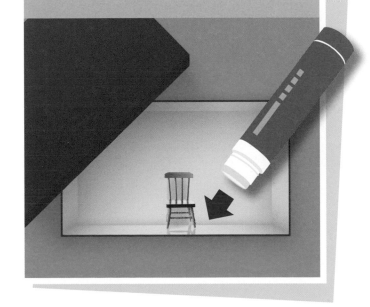

❷ Turn the shoebox on its side. Glue items on this new bottom in the same way. Now which way is up?

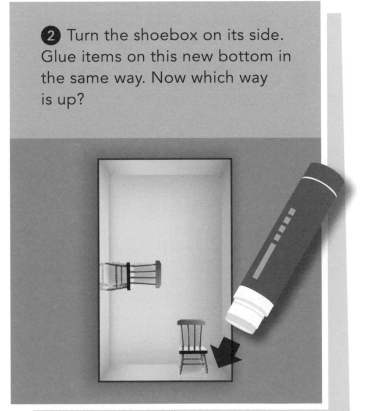

IMPOSSIBLE TRIDENT

Run your fingers over these **impossible objects**. Can you make sense of them? They're unbelievable!

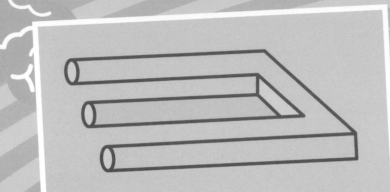

Count the prongs at the end of this fork. Now count the prongs attached to the handle. Are they the same number?

WOW! WHAT'S HAPPENING?

You should count three prongs at the end of the fork, but only two attached to the handle. This is known as the impossible fork, or trident. The outer edges of the pointed prongs become the inner edges at the other end. This impossible drawing style works for other objects too: long bars, pillars, and even animals!

Draw an impossible elephant. How many legs can you count?

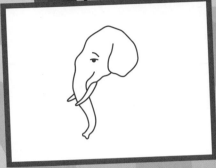

1 Draw an elephant's head with a large ear, one eye, two tusks, and a long curved trunk hanging down to the ground.

2 Draw the elephant's body, starting behind the ear and wrapping around to the elephant's back leg. Add the belly and the top of a front leg only.

3 Use the lines you started to draw for the front leg to create two other legs, as shown.

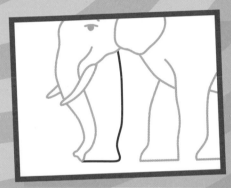

4 Draw a leg directly behind the trunk, using the back of the trunk as the front part of the leg.

5 Draw a leg just in front of the rear leg, as shown. This is in a normal position, but it becomes a fifth leg for this impossible elephant!

ANIMAL TANGLES

Similar to the impossible fork, these animal pictures just don't work.
You can't make **heads or tails** of them!

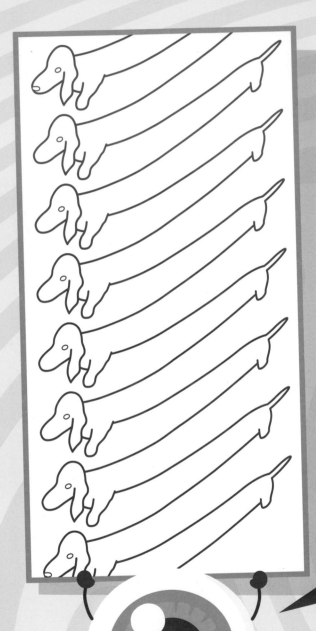

Try coloring in the dogs and cats on this page. What happens?

WOW! WHAT'S HAPPENING?

When you try to color in these creatures, you should discover that the heads and tails are not lined up. They are, in fact, next to each other! At a glance, the pictures work because you expect them to, and the many lines confuse your brain. But up close, you notice that they're not right at all!

Trace the dotted lines to make your own animal trickery picture. Draw in some snake eyes, too!

WOW! WHAT'S HAPPENING?

Look closely at this picture based on art by René Magritte. Is the horse between the trees or in front of them? Or both? The artist plays with your expectations of how the picture should look in order to bewilder your brain.

63

TWO-HEADED TRICKS

They say two heads are better than one … But is that true when there's only one body? See what you think about these **impossible pictures**.

WOW! WHAT'S HAPPENING?

The angle of the camera makes it look like these animals have two heads! You know that can't be true, but the point of view makes you do a double take. In fact, one body is hidden almost perfectly behind the other.

Try this great photo optical illusion with the help of some friends.

1 Ask one friend to stand straight in front of you, the photographer.

2 Then ask your other friends to hide behind the first person and stick out their arms in different directions. Make sure no other bodies or heads can be seen when you take the picture!

65

PHOTO FOOLERY

Cameras, mirrors, and extra people can be positioned just right to fool you. These impossible photos are **picture perfect**!

WOW! WHAT'S HAPPENING?

Clever photographic tricks can create all kinds of impossible photos. In the first photo, a second boy is likely to be buried in the sand, but your brain sees this picture as a boy holding his own head! And in the two photos on the right, a mirror reflects the background just right to replace the top girl's body and bottom girl's face, making each look like she's missing something.

Spot the odd one out in these odd pictures.

WATER WIZARDRY

You can see the impossible in real life, too. Try these tricks to experience the **wizardry** for yourself!

WOW! WHAT'S HAPPENING?

This impossible optical illusion is actually totally explainable by science. Rays of light slow down as they travel from air to water, the same as how we walk more slowly in water. The rays bend, making your pencil look bent, too!

Place a pencil in a clear glass of water. Do you notice how the pencil suddenly looks disjointed?

Make an arrow change direction! For this trick, you'll need a piece of cardstock, a black felt-tip pen, a clear glass, and a pitcher of water.

1 With the felt-tip pen, draw a thick arrow pointing to the left on your piece of cardstock.

2 Hold the cardstock straight up behind the glass. Stand or kneel so that you're looking directly at the arrow.

3 Ask an adult to pour water slowly from the pitcher into the glass.

4 As the water rises above the arrow behind, what do you see? The arrow should suddenly change direction!

ART DISTORTION

Artists play with **perspective and point of view** to create some paintings that look very odd when viewed head on—but come together into a perfect picture from just the right angle!

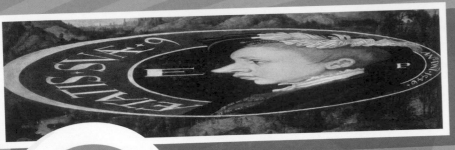

WOW! WHAT'S HAPPENING?

This old painting looks very distorted when viewed front-on. But from the side, it appears normal!

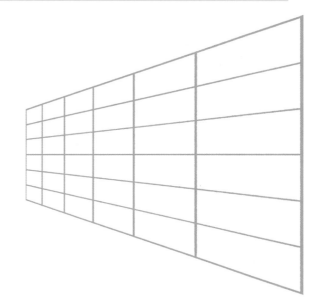

Copy this lion head onto the stretched grid, stretching your lines to fit each matching square. Now look at the picture from the smallest side. Does it still look distorted?

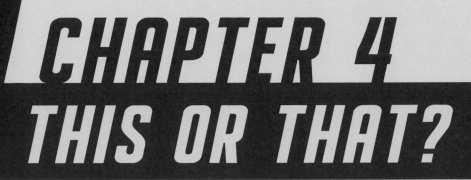

CHAPTER 4
THIS OR THAT?

This chapter is full of puzzling pictures. Some have different images within the same picture, some combine separate images into one, and some just need to be turned upside down! It all depends on your focus ... Will you see this—or that?

DUCK OR RABBIT?

In this **classic this-or-that** image, you can see two different animals depending on your focus. Try making the same illusion with shadow puppets to quack up your friends!

What animal do you see facing to the left? And what do you see facing to the right?

WOW! WHAT'S HAPPENING?

Your brain can't process two images at the same time, so it flips back and forth between the two. First it sees a duck, then a rabbit, then a duck, then a rabbit ... and so on!

Create the same illusion using your hands and shadows.

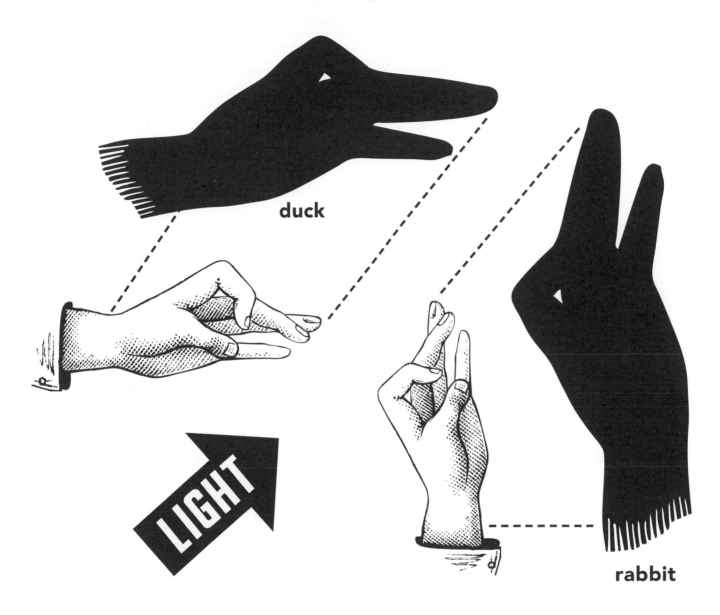

duck

rabbit

LIGHT

1 Shine a light toward a wall. Place your hand in front of the light and copy the finger positions above to make a duck.

2 Keeping your fingers in the same position, turn your hand so that your arm is straight up. The duck has become a rabbit!

3 Now, try out this shadow puppet on a friend. Can they guess what animal it is?

YOUNG OR OLD?

In another classic this-or-that illusion, a **young woman** can age in seconds as she morphs into an **old woman** the more your eyes wander over the image.

What do you see in this picture? Can you see an old man or a young couple?

Do you see a young woman looking away, an old woman with a long chin, or both?

WOW! WHAT'S HAPPENING?

These images are designed to look like two things, and your brain might flip between seeing one and then the other as it tries to process them.

This picture is definitely a young woman, right?
Turn the page upside down. Now what do you see?

FACE OR VASE?

This illusion plays with **background and foreground** to confuse your brain. Which is which? Can you face it?

Create a mirror image on the picture below by coloring the shape on the left in black pen. Now what do you see?

How about the image above? Can you see anything other than a vase?

WOW! WHAT'S HAPPENING?

In these images, the vase in the center is carefully designed with sides that look like face profiles (the side-on view of a face). If you look at the vase, the faces blend into the background and the vase stands out. But look at the faces, and suddenly they become the focus while the vase turns into the background and hardly looks like a vase at all.

Can you spot two faces in this tree? How about in the apple core? Circle them.

Can you see faces in the butterfly picture, below?
Look at the bottom of the page if you need a hint to help you.

CAT OR DOG?

This **purr-fect** illusion has smaller images within a larger one. Which do you see?

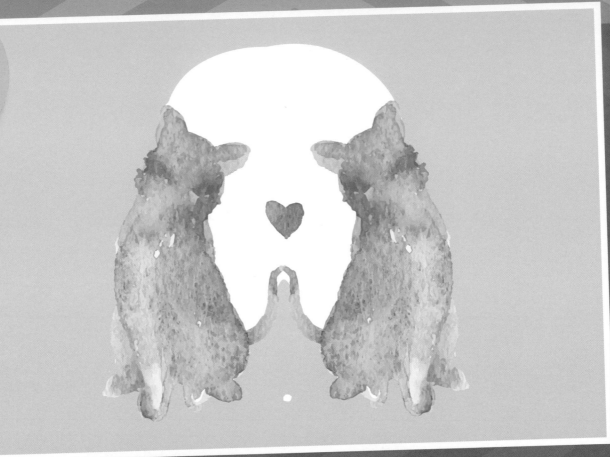

How many cats can you see in this image? How many dogs?

WOW! WHAT'S HAPPENING?

If you focus on this picture as a whole, you should see a dog face looking out at you. But let the white section blend into the background, and suddenly you see two cats leaning in! Once again, your brain flips back and forth between two interpretations of the same image.

*Use the grid to draw the mirror image of this picture.
What shape have you created in the middle?*

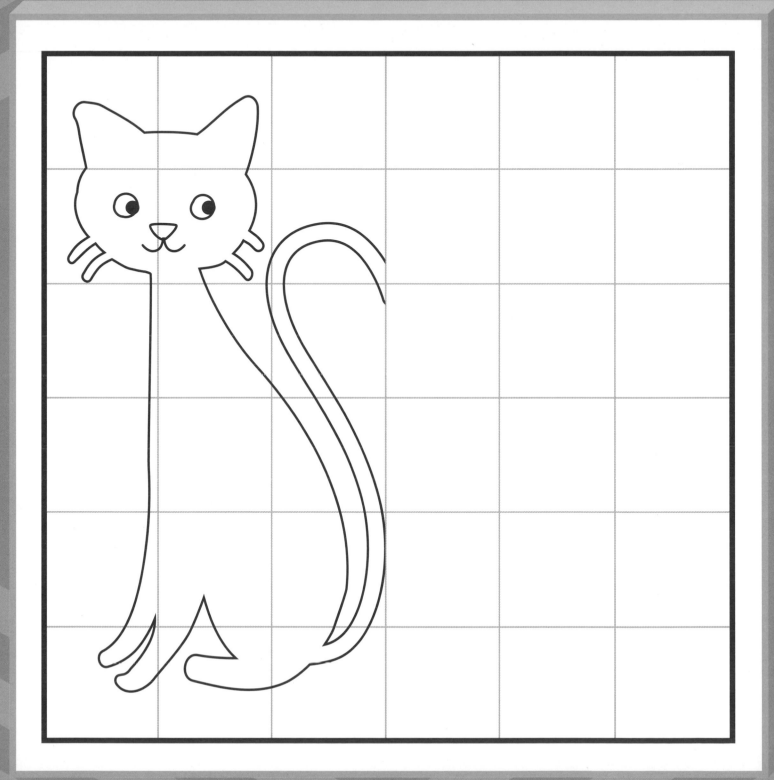

IN OR OUT?

In these images, your focus can change how you see the **angle** of a picture. Try it ...
Are you in or are you out?

Decorate this picture! Does it change how you see the illusion?

Do you see this book's spine coming out of the page? Or is it going into the book, with the pages coming out towards you?

WOW! WHAT'S HAPPENING?

Your brain sees the world in 3-D, so it tries to see pictures that way too. This picture could be either in or out in 3-D, so your brain flips back and forth between the two!

Do you see this face side-on or face-on?

How about the photo below? It's face-on, right? Color over the right side with black pen, as dark as you can, using the line as a guide. Now what do you see?

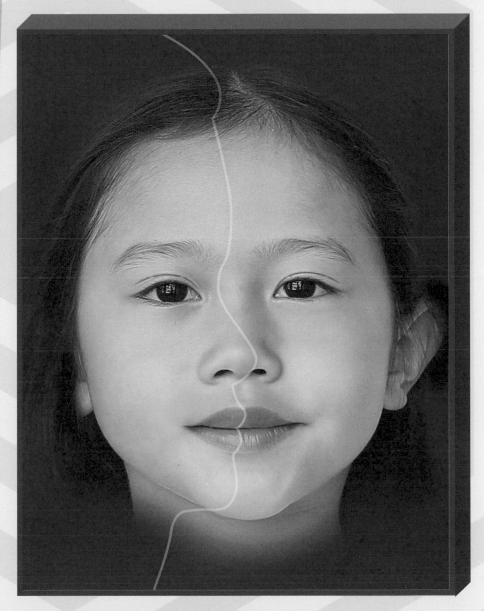

DOUBLE MEANING

These illusions are doubly cool! The art in this room has a **second meaning** when you see it all together from a certain angle—this is because the human brain is programmed to recognize faces in everything!

Find your way through the maze, from the nose down to the bottom of the floorboards.

WOW! WHAT'S HAPPENING?

This room is called The Face of Mae West by famous artist Salvador Dalí. He positioned each individual piece of art, as well as curtains and a strangely shaped red sofa, to make you see a face as you walk into the room.

Design your own illusion art! Find junk, unused objects, and craft supplies around your house. Position them into a shape that makes a face when you look from above. Now take a photo of your creation!

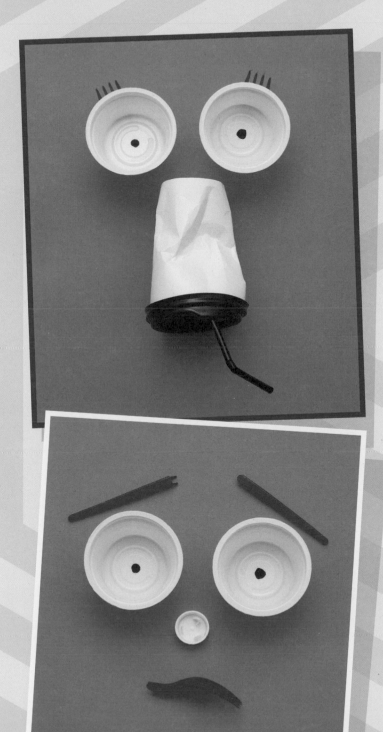

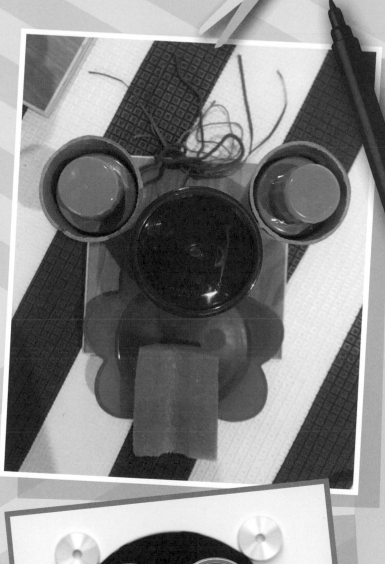

HIDE-AND-SEEK

Some puzzle pictures have **hidden images** within a larger one.
Can you spot them all, or are you totally puzzled?

Not including the fox, there are 15 faces hidden in this
painting. Find and circle them all. Hint: Look closely at
the tree trunks and plants!

WOW! WHAT'S HAPPENING?

*Your brain uses edges to recognize shapes. The edges of
tree trunks, clever shading on plants, and even the spaces
between are designed to reveal hidden pictures in this
painting of The Puzzled Fox by artists Currier and Ives.*

There is a hidden animal in this pretty pattern. Color each shape that has a dot in it to discover who it is!

HAZY HYBRIDS

A **hybrid** is a mix of two things. In this case, photos are combined to put your brain in a haze of confusion. For once, don't look closely ...

Who do you see when you look at this photo? Place the book upright on a shelf or table and walk to the other side of the room. Look at the picture again. Now who do you see?

WOW! WHAT'S HAPPENING?

This image is actually two photos layered on top of each other: a sharp, detailed picture of scientist Albert Einstein and a blurry image of famous actress Marilyn Monroe. Up close, your brain focuses on the sharp details and sees Einstein. But far away, this becomes blurry, and so Marilyn Monroe's features become more obvious.

What animal do you see in this picture? Walk to the other side of the room. Now what animal do you see?

87

THIS AND THAT!

Here is where this OR that becomes **this AND that**! Instead of two images in one picture, here are two pictures that can turn into one.

Hold the book with your arms straight out in front of you. Stare at the space between the birds. Bring the book closer to you slowly, while still staring between the birds. You should eventually see the birds coming together, beaks touching and kissing!

WOW! WHAT'S HAPPENING?

As you move the book closer to your face, the two birds start to move closer together and will eventually overlap. Your eyes can't focus on the two clear images when these images are so close to you!

Turn two images into one with some cardstock and string.

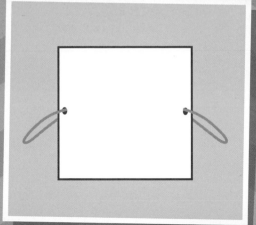

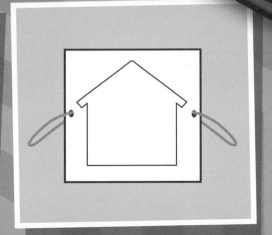

1 Cut your cardstock into a square shape. Punch a hole on the left side and a hole on the right side, as shown.

2 Thread string through one hole and tie it into a loop. Do the same with the other hole, so that you have a second loop.

3 Draw a simple doghouse in the center of one side of the cardstock.

4 Flip the cardstock over vertically. Draw a dog in the center of this side. The doghouse on the other side of the cardstock should look upside down.

5 Twist the strings as tightly as you can. Hold one in each hand, using your thumb and first finger to turn the ends in opposite directions.

6 Pull the strings apart, so that the cardstock spins. Watch closely as the two images seem to become one! The dog should appear in the doghouse.

TRICKS OF THE EYE

So how do all these illusions trick your brain? It's all about playing tricks on the eyes and knowing how they normally work.

See your finger move before your very eyes.

1 Hold one finger straight out in front of you.

2 Cover one eye with the other hand. Look at your finger.

3 Now cover the other eye, without moving your finger or your eyes. Did you see your finger move?

WOW! WHAT'S HAPPENING?

Each of your eyes sees a slightly different view to the other one. So when you use one eye at a time, your view of your finger changes! Lots of illusions play with this fact to make images jump around or confuse you.

You can also play tricks on your eyes using your blind spot. Find yours!

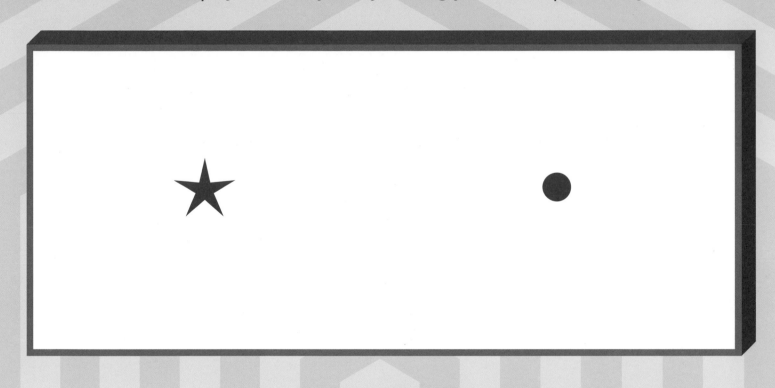

1 Hold the book up close to your face.

2 Cover your left eye. Stare at the dot with your right eye. You should see the star out of the corner of your eye.

3 Slowly move the book away from you, still staring at the dot with your right eye.

4 Notice that the star disappears! That's when it's in your blind spot.

WOW! WHAT'S HAPPENING?

Each of your eyes has a blind spot—a place where it sees nothing. You don't normally notice this, because your two eyes work together and cover each other for a full view of the world. But when you cover one eye, the blind spot is easy to spot!

HIDDEN HEADS

Many illusion artists hide whole faces within their art—you just need to turn the pictures upside down to see them! This is art literally **turned on its head.**

What do you see when you look at this painting? Turn the book upside down. Now what do you see?

WOW! WHAT'S HAPPENING?

Artist Giuseppe Arcimboldo loved to hide heads within his work. In this one, your brain can't imagine an upside-down image of the vegetable bowl, so when you turn the book over, the man's face is a surprise!

ANSWERS

PAGE 8—SPINNING SHAPES

PAGE 18—FLOATING FUN

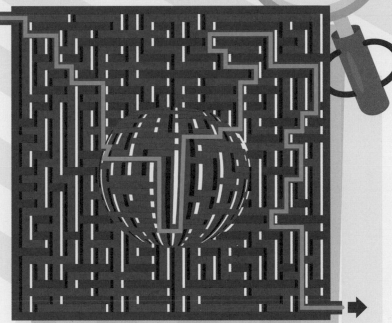

PAGE 22—SHRINKING

PAGE 28—SNEAKY SHAPES

ANSWERS

PAGE 34—SIZE DISGUISE
Each pair of objects is the same size.

PAGE 38—PERSPECTIVE POWER
The men are the same size.

PAGE 45—PHONY FACES

PAGE 67—PHOTO FOOLERY
The odd one out is image 4.

PAGE 77—FACE OR VASE?

PAGE 82—DOUBLE MEANING

PAGE 84—HIDE-AND-SEEK

Did you get them all right?

PAGE 85—HIDE-AND-SEEK

Picture credits
The publisher would like to thank the following for permission to reproduce their material:

p24 (bottom) Wikimedia; p57 (bottom) © István Orosz; p60 (bottom left) Mat Edwards; p66 (left) Wikimedia; p70 (top) National Portrait Gallery / Alamy Stock Photos; p72 (bottom right) Wikimedia; p82 Kiev.Victor / shutterstock.com; p84 Glasshouse Images / Alamy Stock Photo; p86 © Aude Oliva; p92 Wikimedia

All other images are Shutterstock.